DYSLEX IN

*Letters without thoughts
are just marks on a page*

Paul Ross

Hello See if you
will Pick up a Pen
and Get in the Ring
with My Through
Care
Paul.

DYSLEXIC THOUGHTS IN WORDS 1

Thoughts, feelings & celebration of my
dyslexic mind

By

Paul Ross

Published by

THOUGHTS IN WORDS PUBLISHING

ISBN number
978-1-910384-05-3

A WRITER IS
JUST
SOMEONE
WHO JUST
WRITES
NO ONE SAID
ANYTHING ABOUT
SPELLING

Hello Reader.
Contained within these pages are small samples of my celebration of thoughts

My name is Paul Hugh Ross, Hugh is the name of my godfather whom I never see, it's a tradition passed down from the family, (not the never seeing part, just the name!)
Turning fifty this year, I'm up to my neck in mid life revelations. I had been to at least eleven schools by the age of thirteen, lived in numerous parts of Southampton, passed from aunty to uncle, ripped from Southampton to London, London to Southampton then back to London. That's what you get when your family are publicans.
At the age of thirteen they were told I was completely illiterate, something I knew all along. With the help of my family, school and my own inclination, I entered adult education as a complete illiterate, a week after my first angel was born. Wanting just to be able to read a book to my daughter at bedtime and with one to one help from ladies (whose names I have forgotten but will never forget their help and kindness)
 I can now read with my spelling still "well over the rainbow" springs to mind.

I believe all we can do in life is

Agree
Disagree
Or foolishly think
we can go through life without taking part

So here we go....

I am Dyslexic. Dyslexia is a word I feel gets banded around without people really understanding the true meaning of the word. Everyone knows the name but how many have seen its true colours?

My mind has always been a rainbow of colours, on full speed, with the only constant being my loving wife. I write, then she, with the patience of a Saint, goes over each word so my thoughts can be heard when I am not there **"But as this is my book I thought I would let you see just a little more of my colours"** - so please do not feel alarmed if you see and find different ways of using these letters.

By using your SMARTPHONE and download a FREE BAR CODE APP you can see a whole lot more.

Authors

&

Paul Ross

MY ILLITERATE BRITISH LIBRARY

05.12.2007

I am insignificant

Sitting having a coffee in a world of words

Leaves fall like the history of our time

With the thoughts of a King by my side

No one with eyes to read could see the
devastation

Binding nature away from the sun

Away from the rain and wind

Ripping flesh to serve just our thoughts and
deeds

No one with eyes to read could ever think I
made sense

But my eyes were first opened without your eyes

And within this learned place l now sit

Feeling the massacre of trees

ANGEL

2005
Never fall in love with an angel.
With the intention of folding their wings.

IF YOUR WRITE YOUR THOUGHTS
DOWN IN A DIFFERENT DIRECTION.

COULD YOU SEE YOUR THOUGHTS FROM
A DIFFERENT DIRECTION

BAD TO GOOD

I CAN'T IS A CHALLENGE

THE SMARTEST PART OF ME
IS FLESH AND BONE

I CAN'T SPELL - BUT I CAN WRITE

William Shakespear You Are
Stupid, As Thick As Two Short Planks

I am no William Shakespear but my spelling is the ssame, my mind flys with dreams and colours as hes did then.

Some would say William Shakespears thoughts are art placed upon the page but if you really look at William Shakespears HAND WRITING you will see that the spelling is not constant throughout its length and his life. Its only now looking back we see this, but could I argued that he was a dyslexic of his onw time. Dyslexica never started when we start reading and writing book, it was only labels then. It was there within our minds before we started writing, I would say "its the way we think".

Is the thought the art that is the most important think? Its only now when we are restricked to writing within a framework that the art can be lost as people consider more about the framework of the peace and less on it content. I think some still tell kids this by there words, actions and laberling. I do find it wherd how so many people who have read his work dismiss his spelling over the content of his words. But over the years in schools teachers have mist content by conforming to the spelling.

I remember the first story I ever rote, I couldn't have been more then seven/eight but the teacher asked the class to write a storie, so I wrote a seven/eight year olds story, OK it may not have been a work of art but when the teacher ask who would like to stand and tell there story to the class my hand was the first to the sky and up I stood. I can't remember the words or even how the story whent but the smiles I can remember and the teachers words "well done Paul come over to my desk so I can mark it". Thoughs words still finds a place at the middle of my back like a nail being pushed throw my spine. She liked the story, she said she did, she like it enugh to mark in good. But when my page left my hand and entered the world of words upon a page my teacher rolled it up very small and throw it in the bin like a little ball. "I'm sorry Paul you can not write so just sit back down at your besk and you will start all over again".

My mind is starting to think. If you lable people with being dyslexic as having a problem, or any of the other words that can restrict their minds with mental bars they then have to push throw even befor doing anything, instead of saying its OK, just let go of your thoughts.
To me letters without thought are just marks on a page. We should all take a leaf from William Shakepears writings. Just write don't care about the spelling, conformity or structor, just write to get your thoughts out. Don't be scared, restricted by the bars that have been placed within your mind by rools and the words of others. These can be nails that pin your mind to the floor. If nothing ells, if someone asks you

to tell your story stand up proud as every part of us, the good, bad, easey and hard is our story....
I know kids are self conscious but one thing I would have liked to have had in school was being asked to write my thoughts down at home on a topic, story or poem knowing everyone in the class would have to do the same and say, tell or perform there thoughts the next day in class. Then you may see the ture essence of the person and what they truly think without the restrictions of nailed down thinking, "I have to write this spelling correctly". Problems come when my first thoughts are, I must try to conform, put my spelling right, I can't, will it be ok. These thoughts can overwhelm amd take the place off fluwidity, thoughs gorges thoughts of gental arcking rainbow in my mind have, now disaperd, scard of by trying to conform.

What I'm trying to say is if William Shakespear was born now with all the restrictions placed on the spelling, conformity of wards and labelling , world he ever have get past feeling inabiquet as a kid to even come up with the amazing, bueatifal, constructive thoughts as an adolt?
I truly believe if he was in my class at school the teacher would have singled him out like I have seen with others and me, simply saying -

"William Shakespear you are stupid, as thick as two short planks"...

IN THIS BOOK NEVER CARE
WHAT OTHERS THINK,

WRITE EVERYTHING BUT PLEASE
NOT A SHOPPING LIST :)

DEAD SOLDIERS

21.10.2008
We see a glimpse on the telly as they pass
Just a quick glimpse on the telly
As they pass from our thoughts
Another number on the list growing longer
As our hearts become harder
To the tears of the Mother's never seen
Just a glimpse on the telly as our life goes on.
Changing hearts and minds is what the
politicians say
But can changing hearts and minds over there
Be changing hearts and minds over here?
Just a glimpse On the telly
of coffins coming home is not enough To show
Our gratitude and Horror of young lives taken

For me books are just to tell a store when the writer is not in the room or die.

I have listened to a nough dyslexic's to know we all have amazing thoughts and minds.
But any thoughts exsprested no matter how others may perseave them must be better than holding your thoughts to close so no one will see your store.

So if I am not to bold, please take a breath then a pen and answer this. Whats your story?

RASTA MAN

30.01.2006

A giant Rasta crossed my path the other day,
Brilliant colours he wore
Shone bright on the pavement of rainbow greys.
With an elegance and grace I had never seen
before
So slow, sure and graceful within that Rasta's
walk
Like silk being rolled to the floor. And I
some would say, fat white cracker dude
I was transfixed, in awe.
He spotted me looking and stood very still
With no grimace or smile His voice broke
through;
Hey! What are you looking at, ya you looking at
me?
Would he believe I saw the gracefulness within
his movement
The proud-ness in his eyes, his spirit held so
deep inside
But before I could answer, before I could say
This Rasta shook his head slowly giving me the
finger
He turned. He walked away
My mind shouted. No!! Don't get the wrong idea
But the lights had turned to green
And the horns behind me started to sing
And life, my life must go on.

I am not a religious man but I did pray that night
I prayed if a man has the strength to ask a
question
Have the strength to wait for the answer.

PANDA

10.07.2006
Without black eyes
Panda's are not Panda's
With black eyes
Children lose their childhood
I hope you laugh
At the Panda's
I hope you do more than shed a tear
Then forget the Child
For in time your conscience will find you
And then you may truly know
The regret of your heart
Cold, Empty, dead
To the joy and warmth
Of Panda's eyes
And your hart
Full of life
Full of light
Full of colour
Fully grown

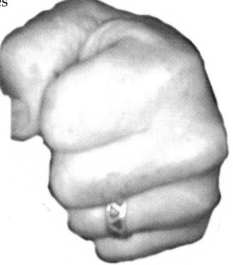

WHAT WAS THAT?

2005
Grasping one raindrop from within a shower
Can be easier than holding a thought
While finding a pen.

A MAD MAN 100 YEARS AGO COULD KILL 9u
HIS SELF AND AS FAR AS A HORSE COULD
CARRY HIM - NOW HE CAN RIDE THE
WINDS OF THE WORLD.

REMEMBER WE SHOULD WORK TO LIVE AND NEVER
LIVE FOR WORK.

LIVE TO WORK, NO, N°,
* WORK TO LIVE "YES". YES

DID PRACTICING RAINDROPS GIVE
US THE WORD. RAIN?

GENIUS SOMETIMES
CAN JE JUST TIME AGAINST
AGE.

THOUGHTS ARE LIKE A RAIN DROPS IF YOU
WANT TO KEEP IT PUT OUT YOUR HAND
AND GRASP IT TO FIND
IT PR TO FIND IT IN
A RIVER IS HARDER.

FASHION

02.09.2006
Some things have returned to fashion,
Some thingssI look forward to
This one has vexed me all my life -
The one that looks good on you for we took this
fashion.
We thought it was cool, we thought it was cool
To look like you.
This is the one that I do hate
But please never think I would ever denigrate.
For you see I was borne in the sixties
So the hippies, caftans, free love and pot all
passed me by, shit
Glam rock sparkled, siquins and lipstick in the
seventy
And believe me some of thoughs Cats Did have
feathers in their hair but At 14, I was too scared
to try
It hung on until the eighties
Then in the eighties it began to die
Thank God it began to die
But now they have returned.
You can see them every day
You can see them on street corners
In every shape and size

But let me now lay out my thoughts
And say what I have been trying to say
To me, you see just to me -
Afros have always looked good on black men
Perms have always looked shit on whites.

DRAWING THOUGHTS

Take That Bullet, Blow Their Minds

02/03/2014
Man I know wanted
Gun and bullet, bullet and gun
Gun and bullet, bullet and gun!
What the f--k!

His mind clouded
no turned cheek
drowning in red mist seae's,
I'll get there family signing names on f—king
granite, he promises me!

My screaming thoughts, must calm before words
Don't sign yours too, see through this
See the history of our time and remember
One bullet can only go so far
Blowing one mind as it go's
But a bullet of thought
Fired through words can encompass the world
Blowing all minds as it go's

PARADISE

25.011.2008
Could Heaven be the place you abandon all
morality
Just leave it all at the door
Quench your desires and lust in abandonment
Pluck all the apples from the heavenly tree, not
just one
Drenching your soul in a hedonistic sea
Fornicating with painted souls
With never a thought for blame or care
Love for just love's sake
Without eyes to judge or see
For what the hell are seventy-two virgins for?
And if that is the case
Could hell be just a place
Where God has rounded up all the sinners
Just to make them all
Go to church.

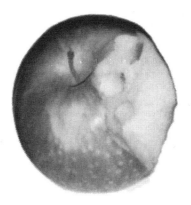

THE NATURAL ORDER

13.12.2008
My beliefs are
The natural order of the universe is
Black,
Silent,
Still
And it is only in chaos that we find the creation
of
Light
Sound
Movement
For as we all know
Each star will burn out in time
And sound
Sound is just the movement from and back to
silence
Like waves upon the sand
As for stillness and movement
In stillness alone
I find peace.

DARK FATHER

2005

I should have stood above you father while you were still
asleep
Holding a cricket bat in one hand, and your bruise upon
my cheek
I should have slowly woken you from your happy
slumber
Explaining as calmly as I could
I never asked to be here
I was just born into this place
I would have loved to love you father
Not the bully in his place
Have your loving arms surround me
Not just your fists for laying down the laor
Loved to have you walk beside me
Not kicking me once I had been hammered to the floor
"I love you son" is all I wanted
Not the bruise, not the screams, not the tears
But then to thank you, for I must thank you
For all the teaching you bestowed
Never run away or cowl,
stand strong, stand proud, just win, never ever be put
down
Then to tell him that I know
At thirteen I was never the match for him
Then to tell him it all will stop, no matter what the cause
For he would never sleep well at night
Without locking all his doors
As he has stripped the youth from his son
As the father was to his son, no one
I love him now, but in my own way
When I was twenty-one, he died
Before I had time to tell him
All the nightmares I had kept locked inside

Up until the day at forty-one when I let him go on this
page
He ruled my mind in anger, I kept him locked away
But now he is out and to the pages he has gone
And I pray in time my memories will decay.

LIKE A SKY DIVER, LETTING GO IS THE HARDEST THING
LETTING GO OF YOUR THOUGHTS CAN BE TERRIFYING BUT
ONCE YOU HAVE IS ~~EXALTHE~~ EXHILARATING

WELL SOMETHING LIKE THAT.

BODY ROULETTE

01.2006
I wish to fart
I know I do
To let one squeeze
so proudly through
I would place good money upon that fart
As the best that money can buy
But the odds you see, The odds
You must always be sure to think of the odds
For believe me, that is all that counts.
The late night curry
The gallons of beer
Could the odds be
That fart will not appear?
I feel the only way to win this game
Is definitely not to play
So now I sit upon this throne of mine
Shit!
I've lost my bet
But hey,
I feel fine.

YOU COULD NEEL?

24.02.2008

I pray the regrets that we will have
As we pass from this life,
Will only be the regrets
We can live with.

MIND TWISTED

24.04.2007

I am troubled
For how can my thoughts
Be troubled by my thoughts?
But my thoughts
Are troubled by my thoughts
For is the real me
The one who thinks of things to do,
The one who does the things I think -
Or
The one who has the strength
To say
No?

THE DEVILS PRAYER

12.09.2008
The Devils prayer must be
"Mankind survive"
"Mankind survive"
"Mankind survive"
For how can he play with nothing?

ME

My body is scraped and scarred from the
labours of my life
My hair is slowly receding. Just another thing to
place
On the black board of my age
But when you look at me, do you see me in a
pub?
Or with my broken nose as a door man
You're not coming in, love.
Am I standing on the terrace screaming at the
Ref?
Am I standing in a ring with blood strewn down
my chest?
You must have played Rugby are the words I
often hear
You see the shell that I inhabit has worked hard
all its life
Yes, the shell that I inhabit has had its bit of
strife
But you don't see my elegance as it's not
sculptured on my face
But my elegance will last my life time not crack,
as age comes to feast
If I just stood without my thoughts being
expressed by words
If I just stood before you then only my shell you
would observe.

Iike a book all you would see is the cover
But with a book you would take time to discover
Would you then read the outside then look within?
Hoping the story will unfold like no other
But do you do that for me, do you ever take that time?
One thing to remember as you read through the body of those books;
They can be handed down from Granddad to grandson
Grandma to granddaughter
Don't you understand books are time travellers, we are stuck in time.
Our lives are short so take the time to know and live with each other.
If you want to ask a question ask a neighbour before diving to a book
For information shared means we are talking with each other.
Talking comes from within the shell from behind your eyes that have judged.
To see the real me I hope will shatter all your thoughts.
I hope the colours of my life blind your eyes
So your soul will look instead.
 For three strings make my bow
 And just three strings are what make us whole
Mind, Body, Soul.

How do you see you?

MONKEYS

01.11.2006
Do monkeys think we're crazy?
The way we live our lives
Changing the air we breathe to grey
Obliterating land and skies
Digging great holes to bring up stones,
For to them
Is a stone just a stone just a stone?
I feel a question must be asked
Before we can all go on,
Are we really happier than the monkeys?
That feed upon roots and leaves
They sit proudly on their lofty trees
Looking down at me.
Could monkeys call us monkeys
Then call themselves Mankind?

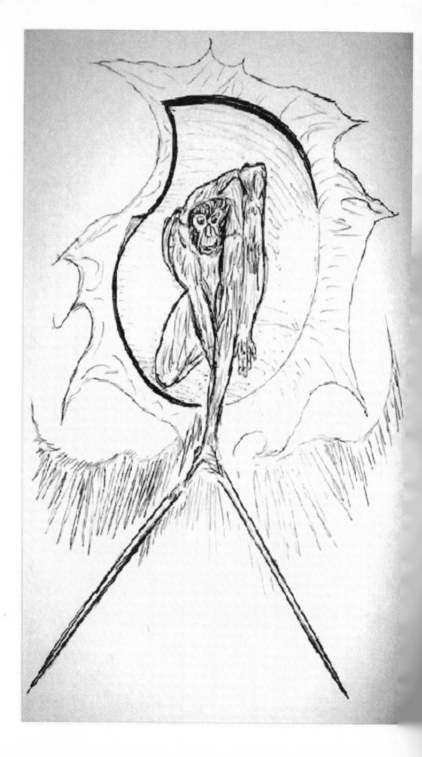

DOGS DINNER

27.11.2006

A dog is not just for Christmas
With a little love and care
And extra vegetables

It can last you through
New years too

GOLD FISH

15.03.2009
Are we restricted by the way we manipulate our
five senses?
Dancing within that framework of five
Manipulating the world around us
For I know from the their feedback
I'm in a plane in flight
Within the five, we have been told,
Have faith in God as we are created in his image.
Have you agreed with my thoughts?
If you have, would you please answer this:
Within the restrictions of these senses
Can all life be sentient?
For within its world
I cannot believe a goldfish believes itself to be
stupid
And now a question comes to my dome
Within its own world
Dose the goldfish have faith in God
Knowing God is created in MY image?

EGGS FOR ME

21.02.2006
A plain yogurt for you bacon and eggs for me
Skimmed milk in your coffee full fat in mine
please
And can I have that last sausage
On your plate you will never eat, as the taste is
delish
And the fat is ow so sweet
You, a canderel spec, three sugars in my tea
My late night kebabs potato couching in front of
the TV
You never said no you just let me live my life,
thanks
Your two hundred sit-ups each morning
As I'm scratching at my crutch
These are the things I remember so much
I am so sorry the car didn't give a toss
Of the way you had suffered to live your lot
The drunk driver never gave a fig
Gracefully arching you to the sky
No clouds that day, deep blue as far as you
could see
A sunshine day you called it, You so sweet in
every way
Your grace finished, on contact with the
pavement
No screams. No movement. No life. No me.
Just a six months ban and he celebrates in my
local for not going down "?"

THE SCHOLAR

2007
You are an English scholar standing in a
bookshop
With the world at your finger tips
All you hAave to do is pluck a leaf to
read
All the times that have passed
To all the dreams yet to come
 But the bookshop is located in France
And all you can read is English

From a frustrated dyslexic

Now can you try and

understand?

HAY UN PROFESOR DE LINGLÉS DE PIE EN UNA LIBRERIA
CON EL MUNDO A SUS PUNTAS DE LOS DEDOS
SIN ENBARGO. LA LIBRERIA ESTA DE PIE EN FRANCIA
Y TODO LO QUE EL MAESTRO PUEDE LEER ES EL INGLÉS
DESDE EL FRUSTRADO DISLÉXICOS
¿ENTIENDES AHORA

WILLIAM BLAKE

23.05.2006
I never thought I'd feel this way
to sit around a pond with you
Having your thoughts envelop my soul
You could have never known the stone you
throw
on the oceans of time would bring ripples to sit
with me now
Most ripples start with a climax then subside to
nothing in time
But yours have grown stronger from shallower
times when they did not know
You believed your brother lifted from his body
that become cold
And the joy on his face showed there could be a
place
where all of us may go
In my innocence of youth I found your paintings
but did not know and was unable to read your
wards
With experience I've found you again
Your grace and beauty now observed
With no daughters or sons you could have
believed
your line would lose its light in time
But your wards will be there when time is at rest
as a light that worms our souls

So out goes my hand to shake yours dear
William
to thank you for the colours you bring
Your wards Your pictures
Have brought you to me
And with you my thoughts now sing

~~KNOWLEDGE IS LIFE~~ 23 MAY 06

WILLIAM   AND

(GOD I NEVER THOUGHT I WOULD REACH   So out
THIS WAY   DEAR
TO SIT AROUND A ~~POOL~~ POND WITH YOU   FOR YO
TO LET YOUR ~~WATER~~ WORDS   AGAIN
ENVELOP ME SO   AND WITH
YOU COULD HAVE NEVER KNOW   WILL
THE STONE YOU THREW ~~THEN~~ ON THIS OCEAN OF TIME
WOULD BRING RIPPLES ~~THOUGH~~ ~~FROM~~
TO SIT WITH ME ~~HERE~~ NOW
MOST RIPPLES THEY FADE
BUT ~~YOURS PRIME~~ GROUND STRONGER AND NE PADDED IN THE PAST
~~→~~ YOU BELIEVED ~~MURDERED~~
    YOU ~~BROTHER~~ LIFTED FROM THE ~~~~ BODY
    THAT HAD BECOME COLD
    AND THE JOY ON HIS FACE SHOWED YOU
    ~~YES~~ THERE COULD BE A PLACE MY   GO
    WHERE ALL OF US ~~BOUND TO~~ WILL ~~BE FREE~~
    THE   OR ~~YOUTH~~ ~~REWIND~~
    IN, INNOCENCE, I ~~SEE~~ YOUR PAINTING
    BUT WAS UNABLE TO READ YOUR WORDS
    WITH EXPERIENCE I HAVE READ YOU AGAIN
    YOUR GENIUS AND PURITY NOW OBSERVED
    YOU WILL TRAVEL THROUGH TIME DEAR WILLIAM
    AS LONG AS THERE'S EYES TO ~~READ~~ SEE

WITH
~~AND PEOPLE WANTS~~ NO DATES OR SOUNDS
YOU COULD HAVE BELIEVED YOUR ~~THEORY~~
LINE WOULD ~~FROM~~ NOT GO ON
BUT YOUR WORD WILL BE HERE
WHEN TIME ~~OCEANS~~ RESTED

FRAGILE

28.04.2006

It is always easier
To replace a damaged glass than to repair
it
But the fragile memories
we have sipped are worth trying to repair
Before the good memories we've shared
are forever shattered.

SWEET TOOTH

11.09.2006
Some people come in giving
Some in receiving
Some by not taking part
Some by watching the art
But is it the come we all are seeking?
The sweetness of total let go
For if the brain has come be it pleasure or pain
Is the ecstasy to the brain all the same?
For we all hold back till we can hold back no
more
Then wait for the hit like a brick laying bitch
As our brain can do nothing except let go
And our bodies just exsplodes
The ride we get we know will be over so quick
But there's no ride at Thorpe Park to compare
As the one we give to our brains my friends
When we come without any Shame
 HELL YA!!!

DO WE REALLY NEED MORE

02.2013
Are all the other words
Found in dictionaries so thick
Just the size of waves upon the shores of
Yes, No, Love, Hate ?

FROM KING TO MAN

2005

The Kings words:
I came,
I saw,
I concurred.

Some men's words:

I saw,
I concurred,
I came.

FAITH

23.09.2007

The faiths at speaker's corner all shouting they
are the ones
The one who can save me from my self
If I would just believe in the one
But witch one is the right one?
For they all say theirs is the only right path
Screaming that Allah will save me
Or Christ will rise with my faith
If I would spread the ward
I am truly happy that their faith is a comfort to
them
But for me no flexibility in a book that is static in
time
That was written two thousand years a go
I cannot restrict the thoughts in my mind
Just to live my life in peace and not be roiled
By someone's interpretations of ink
See that is where it falls for me
As the ground splits in my mind to show the
vast divide
For am I on an island where it's OK to believe
That belief's do not necessarily need to be judge
as fact.

BOXER

23.07.2007

The bell sounded as I entered the ring
You were waiting for me
The first punch came on seeing you there
As I instinctively blocked it, I turned it away
The jabs came then on hearing an angel's voice
Air was moved with her song
Within my mind I weaved right then left
As the onslaught and ferocity of body blows
grow
Ducking and moving out from that space
As my body exited that holy place
Then there was calm
I could breathe again
As the knot in my heart relaxed
The uppercut came right out of the blue
For I hugged and kissed your son
Told him I loved him then just looked up
I saw you
Nowhere to run, No where to hide.
Death of my Nan

TORMENT

21.05.2012

Do we all have to go though torment
To become the person we want to be?
For conformity to me
Is one tear in a sea of sweet eternity
Hundred and fifty years ago
Conformity had slave boats crossing the sea,
And just forty years ago
Conformity had laws to imprison consenting
lovers.
Changing conformity can start with just one
voice
Stopping torment allowing thoughts to become
free
Then conformity to me is just a fluid state
Only becoming the way we live
By our actions
Or apathy.

MY WIFE

04.2006
Could I understand the real gravity
Of the words I shouted then?
Really understand the meaning
And what that would truly mean to me now?
We are so quick to think our minds old
When we are still so young
That is the dilemma that befalls everyone
All we had back then was a mind of good
intentions
Only in time we will truly know
Will the promises we make last a life time or just
one day?
We will live and we will grow
We may have children of our own
What is true, is the living of life
Will mold and change us
Each scar and each wrinkle is a store of life
Only mine, for I am all that I have
Its only now I can turn to you true
Understanding the gravity and the meaning
That only in reflection
Off all my good intentions
I am so blessed
To still be with you

SPEAK

06.05.2006

I can speak my dreams to strangers
I can stand on a hill top and scream
Of all the wonders in my mind
You have never seen
But in my breams you are standing beside me
And on the hill top I pray you where there
All the wonders in my mind I have not told you
And I wonder why you do not care
I then held your hand and tool a beep breathe
And speak my breams allowed
For you to see the reel me
Is all I have now
Screams of wonder with you beside me
for on my hill top you open your mind
Your breams
Your wonders
Your desires
For now we have leant to speak of things that
matter
And not just speak our live away
Remembered the wonder of each other
And within each other's dreams
We now play.

A Blank page can have some running for covers, so running for pens.

LEGO BRICKS

2013
They say life is what we make it, so
No shoes + wet grass + have time = smiles.

Always better than just being pissed off in the
rain :)

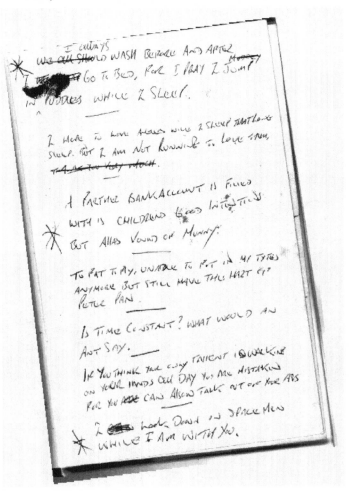

YOUR DREAM KISS

16.03.2007
Your eyes are darkened
From the scarf you have chosen
The touch to your body
Has exploded the sun between your eyes
Your uncontrolled vertebrae now pop from
north to south
Making your spine arch in time with hips
coming forward
To kiss your lover's cheeks
Poetic words have filled your mind
Rainbow colored willow blossom across a
virgins lips
Now you truly understand why poets write
This kiss
This angels caress
Is your entire dream fulfilled
Then with your scarf by your side
Why feel shocked
When you find your lover has bolted
Been caught in young shame
By her Grandma of eighty two
Who has just
Blown you.

FOR ME NOW.

BOOKS AREN'T SCAREY. IT WAS ONLY
THE WAY I LOOKED ON THEM THAT
MADE THEM MY NIGHTMARES.
BUT I NOW LOOK WITH NEW
EYES. AND FOR ME, BOOKS AREN'T
SCAREY ANYMORE.

Have a go taking a pen.

Clear your mind then count to ten, slowly, every number one my one. When a word, thoughts comes to mind just write and keep on going, when your thoughts stops start counting but this time stop whenever a thought popes up.

ETON BRIDGE

19.01.2008
I'm standing between great histories
With the knowledge of our time
A place to make children kings comes to my
mind
Above the artery of our great land
By blood, sweat and toil of the long since past
I'm standing at peace
The protection of three lions to my left
With the strength of knowledge to my right
He over the River Thames between Eaton and
Windsor
On just a bridge I'm standing?

IN MY DARK PLACE

25.04.2006
Is the biggest fight we all must make
The fight within ourselves?
I have always looked out and fought
Always easier than looking in
My self restricted consciousness being shocked
daily at thoughts
Of what my unrestrained subconscious hungers
for
But now l have come to recognize
Without each part I cannot be me
I'm loving, Screaming, Smiling, Happy and Sad
living and learning
To ask the questions of myself
For the first time in my life
Can I forgive myself for things I could not
change?
I stop enlarging each thought?
That should be long since dead
I wipe the darkness of chalk from the slate of my
memories?
Then balance each thought
For the first time Equally with each other
Yes I can, for I have come to recognize this is just
life I know I am not unique we are all made in
flesh and bone
But all of my thoughts are unique to me
My own.

BEHIND CLOSED DOORS

With a world overflowing
In thoughts and dreams
Sick to some is ecstasy.

WE GIVE

We all give the power of Government
To people we believe give a toss
So they can get together and make laws
To hinder the people Who don't give a toss
But the people who don't give a toss, don't give a toss
Then we all have to suffer
When the Government makes new laws
To stamp out those people who don't give a toss
But those people still don't give a toss
This then increases taxes to fund the new laws
That the people who don't give a toss
Will not give a toss about
Now the people who gave a toss
And placed the Government in power
To give a toss on their behalf
Are seeing that the people who don't give a toss
Are getting away with not giving a toss
This has now made the people who give a toss
Left feeling well, -----------------"up set"
So now more people don't give a toss than ever before
And the Government is still making new laws
And taxing us all to the point
That we all don't give a ....

THE OLD HAG

Free writing.

 headmistrase cam into the class and took me out to her office, two mabe 3 other kids where in the tiny room with a old wooded waredrode taking up the hole of the fair wall. We were shore she selpt upside down in there hanging from an oversized coat rale. Write children I'm going to teach you all how to read and write as she took out page, pencils and these bloody PETER AND JANE books from her besk she could darly get round. So for the next (what seemed like years) school term aster are school binnors we all reported to the heads small office to read and write. Some gotto grips with the idear better than others and started to imaging there way out of the room on the stores of thoughs bloody Peter and Jane, some others, well me and someone ells I'm shore there was someone ells, lets just say there was someone ells. ☺ WE took to exspressing how thoughts over the pages with rainbow colourd pencils i had in my satchal, Jane, if my memorl service me right is lookd good with a lovely pink mostash and thick purpol rimmed glasses. And of couse some obligatery black teeth. We the old hag after asking the otheres to leace her room took to having a fit of disapointment at what I or we had done... trying to exsplain how books are sacret thinks, sorry old hag at that time as you were very tale to me the wards just floow right over my head and out through the cracks in the closed door. I remember saying something that got me the slipper, it must have been creative but allas the thought lets with the feeling of hatetred at being hit with the slipper. For the next two weeks I thing the old hag would only see me in her office at break times, no play for me just office at break times. She would explain each time that some "meaning me" would never be able to read or write properly but that is ffine as we need other scills too. So every day there same word, NOT WORDS but word I woukld have to learn and spell, the old hag would come into the class and get me to stand up and try and spell this ward day after day untill after around two weeks of morning and afternoon breack times being stuck in a room with the old hag how lived upside down in a warebrode I could and would remember it. Told to stand and spell it in class, dinnor hall, PE every time was a winner too. Then to her office one day she said, you know what I have done to you. I remember saying, making my life hell. I remember her smile craking her face, now you can spell

EVERYTHING you can do anything, I hatterd
her then, Love her now...

Whats your everything?

Tiptoe on Leaves

05.12.2007
The anger has long gone
With tears returned to earth
Feelings of being apart
Hollow
Never overflowing just half full
Inadequate, stupid, thick as two short planks
Apart from life apart from you
No more

You see I now tiptoe through books
Like you tiptoe through the rain
You will always get some on you
For me it's the same
But my mind can get by
With just the smallest of drops
Within the forest of fallen trees

You call them Libraries.

WE ARE THE UNIVERSE

From my blog post 3rd Nov 2013

"Would the universe ever know of me?" was the question a **friend** asked in her time of need....

It has made me see, think, try to feel my own feelings and beliefs as a formal religion has never appealed to me, for me the leap of faith you must have to believe in the word of a god is a leap of faith to believe in the person who is telling you his interpretation of the word of god.

So at around 24.15 from not thinking anything about the day to day running of the universe I read the question from the heart. *"Would the universe ever know of me?" and i was shocked at my answer.*

I believe it would not miss any of us as it would have to have a memory and with all its vast complexity and variations l feel its no more than a ball that's rolling down a hill, the ball has no thoughts on how it is moving or where it has come from or going but it is moving nevertheless.

The only problem with the universe is us, you and me, everyone you know or have ever known. We all have blades of memory, knowing the past and from that predicting the minutes to come.

Out of all the chaos, complexity, diversity in the universe we must be the luckiest or unluckiest group of atoms, all depending on what side of the blade we individually fall to.

Before you scream out animals have memories to, yes they do but not like ours. Theirs l believe is more instinctive. We have that but ours ascends past this to think on others as well as ourselves, art, poetry, hate and love, these things I would suggest are outside, never meant to be, but in all things one time the great ducks of the universe will have to get in a line and we were the lucky or unlucky ones to win the universal lottery and the wining prize, thought.
So with my prize of thoughts I answer the question . We make the universe for we give it name, without us it would be nothing as we are the only eyes that see it. So the universe is made only by each of us and in our minds, our vast depth and heights of imagination and in my universe each star is sacred

And yours would be missed. x

MY ENLIGHTENMENT

I fould the thing that blow my mind was when I re-read what I had written, I thought I wrote one thing then on re-reading and reflection I found I had written something conpleatley different in a lot of ways

So take your time to read and see what you thing

THEN WHEN YOU ARE FINISHED COME JOIN ME ON OUR AUTHERS PAGE

&

Twitter - My Dyslexic Thoughts@PaulRoss13
Face Book @Dyslexic Thoughts in Wards

Website
www.dyslexicthoughtsinwords.com

Here ends BOOK 1 OF MORE,

If you would like to purchase Book 2 Of More,
or for more information on

Book 2 Of More

Or you would just like to register or comment on
my blog, videos and eBooks, books

Please, just scan

Thank you

ACKNOWLEDGEMENTS

I must thank my Queen who is still holding my
hand after thirty two years,
our two angels that grace our lives, a new son in-
law and being called Granddad is amazing.

My dear friend Vito Gentile
who knows and holds my dreams and
nightmares and for saying it's OK to open my
mind

The gracious Sandy Toksvig
Who could never think why! LOL

And, the esteemed writer and poet, Michael
Rosen for his kind words

*'I really enjoyed reading Paul Ross's poems. They
combine expressions of direct feeling and reflection
told in rhythmic patterns that criss-cross through the
poems. He moves from raw experience to speculation
to judgements on life in engaging ways.*

Content

42723636R00054

Made in the USA
Charleston, SC
07 June 2015